OVERVIEW OF
福建概览 FUJIAN

福建省人民政府新闻办公室 编
The Information Office of Fujian Provincial People's Government

海峡出版发行集团 | 海峡书局
THE STRAITS PUBLISHING & DISTRIBUTING GROUP

目录

P4

FUJIAN,
A PROVINCE EMBRACED
BY THE SEA AND THE
MOUNTAINS

1

山海福建

P22

FUJIAN,
A PROVINCE WITH
A RICH CULTURAL
HISTORY

2

人文福建

P52

FUJIAN,
A PROSPEROUS
AND STRONG PROVINCE

3

富强福建

CONTENTS

FUJIAN,
A PROVINCE EMBRACED BY THE SEA AND THE MOUNTAINS

1

山海福建

地理区位 ■■■■
GEOGRAPHICAL LOCATION

福建地处中国东南沿海，位于北纬 23°31′至 28°20′、东经 115°50′至 120°52′之间，东北与浙江毗邻，西北与江西接界，西南与广东相连，东隔台湾海峡与台湾岛相望，东西最大间距约 499 千米，南北最大间距约 530 千米。

Fujian is a province located on the southeastern coast of China, between 23°31′N 115°50′E and 28°20′N 120°52′E. Fujian is bordered by Zhejiang to the northeast, Jiangxi to the northwest, Guangdong to the southwest, and the island of Taiwan across the Taiwan Strait to the east, with a maximum distance between east and west of about 499 kilometers and that between north and south of about 530 kilometers.

福建省在中国的位置图
Location of Fujian Province on China Map

图 例

★ 北京   首都

○ 天津   省级行政中心

──── 未定   国界

──────── 省、自治区、直辖市界

--------- 特别行政区界

1：30 000 000

审图号：GS(2019)1815 号
自然资源部 监制

行政区划
ADMINISTRATIVE DIVISION

　　福建省简称"闽"，是中国省级行政区，辖福州、厦门、漳州、泉州、三明、莆田、南平、龙岩、宁德 9 个设区市和平潭综合实验区，包括 31 个市辖区、11 个县级市、42 个县（含金门县），省会为福州。

　　Fujian Province, or Min for short, is a provincial-level administrative region in China. Under the jurisdiction of Fujian are nine prefectural cities, i.e., Fuzhou (provincial capital), Xiamen, Zhangzhou, Quanzhou, Sanming, Putian, Nanping, Longyan, and Ningde as well as the Pingtan Comprehensive Experimental Zone, with a total of 31 districts, 11 county-level cities, and 42 counties (including Kinmen County).

福建省概略图
Outline Map of Fujian Province

比例尺 1:3 000 000

黄岗山
2160.8
武夷山市
浦城县
光泽县
南平市
松溪县
寿宁县
福鼎市
政和县
柘荣县
邵武市
周宁县
福安市
星仔列岛
建瓯市
屏南县
霞浦县
大渚山
泰宁县
将乐县
顺昌县
建宁县
古田县
宁德市
浮鹰岛
明溪县
(闽南平潭综区)
罗源县
西洋岛
宁化县
三明市
尤溪县
连江县
福州市
北茭塘岛
清流县
闽清县
闽侯县
鳌江岛
粗芦岛
马祖岛
永安市
永泰县
长汀县
连城县
大田县
戴云山
福清市
大练岛
武平县
德化县
平潭综合
实验区
平潭县
海坛岛
龙岩市
漳平市
仙游县
莆田市
南日群岛
南日岛
上杭县
永春县
湄洲岛
华安县
安溪县
惠安县
南安市
泉州市
南靖县
漳州市
晋江市
石狮市
平和县
厦门市
金门县
金门岛
漳浦县
云霄县
诏安县
东山县
东山岛

审图号：闽S〔2021〕24号
福建省制图院 编制
福建省自然资源厅 监制
注：资料截至2021年5月。

地貌特征

GEOMORPHOLOGICAL CHARACTERISTICS

福建境内崇山峻岭，茂林修竹，丘陵连绵，河谷、盆地穿插其间，山地、丘陵占全省总面积的 90% 以上。武夷山脉为福建第一大山脉，长约 550 千米，东北西南走向。主峰黄岗山海拔 2160.8 米，为福建第一峰，也是中国华东地区（除台湾省外）的最高峰。

武夷山千岩万壑锁云烟
Wuyi Mountains Shrouded in Clouds

More than 90% of Fujian's total area is mountains and hills, which are comprised of lofty mountains, flourishing forests, tall bamboo, and undulating hills that are interspersed with river valleys and basins. The Wuyi Mountains, the largest mountain range in Fujian, are about 550 kilometers long and run from northeast to southwest. Its main peak, Mount Huanggang, is 2,160.8 meters high above sea level, making it the highest mountain in Fujian Province and eastern China (excluding Taiwan Province).

福建丹山碧水，山水交融，河流在丘陵间纵横交错，河网密集。大部分河流发源于福建境内，并由福建境内入海。闽江是福建省最大的河流，总长 2959 千米，干流长 577 千米，流域面积达到 6.09 万平方千米，约占福建省总面积的一半。河流年径流量达 1168 亿立方米，居中国华东地区首位。

Fujian is characterized by its well-integrated green mountains and clear waters; the hills are traversed by ravines and rivers, and most rivers flow into the sea from Fujian. The Min River, with a total length of 2,959 kilometers and a main stream length of 577 kilometers, is the longest river in Fujian Province. The watershed area reaches 60900 square kilometers, accounting for about half of the total area of Fujian Province. The annual runoff reaches 116.8 billion cubic meters, ranking first in eastern China.

闽江古田溪流域蜿蜒绵亘
Winding Drainage Basin of Gutian Brook, Min River

宁德白水洋因其独特的地质地貌被誉为"天下绝景，宇宙之谜"
Baishuiyang in Ningde is known as "unique scenery of the world, mystery of the universe" due to its unique geological and geomorphic features

福建海阔港深，海岸线直线长度 535 千米，曲线长度 3752 千米，曲折率中国第一。海域面积 13.6 万平方千米，125 个港湾犹如一颗颗璀璨的蓝宝石，镶嵌在蜿蜒曲折的海岸线上。沿海共有 2214 个岛屿，总面积 1156 平方千米。平潭岛是福建第一大岛，中国第五大岛。

Fujian has a vast sea and deep harbor, with a straight coastline length of 535 kilometers and a curve length of 3752 kilometers, ranking first in China in terms of tortuosity. The sea area is 136000 square kilometers, and 125 bays are like sparkling sapphires embedded in the winding coastline. There are a total of 2214 islands along the coast, with a total area of 1156 square kilometers. Pingtan Island is the largest island in Fujian and the fifth largest island in China.

| 碧海云天，晋江海滩
Blue Sea and Clear Sky Beach in Jinjiang

气候特点 ||

CLIMATE CHARACTERISTICS

福建虽靠近北回归线以北，但西北有武夷山脉阻挡寒风，东南有海风调节，亚热带海洋性季风气候特征显著。气候暖热湿润，大部分地区冬无严寒，夏少酷暑，雨量充沛。年平均气温 15℃～ 22℃，无霜期 250 ～ 330 天，平均降雨量 1400 ～ 2000 毫米，是中国雨量最丰富的省份之一。

Despite its proximity to the Northern Tropic, Fujian is fortunate to have sea breezes from the southeast to regulate the climate and the Wuyi Mountains to the northwest to ward off the cold winds, resulting in a distinctive subtropical oceanic monsoon climate. Fujian is warm and humid, and receives abundant rainfall in most areas. Its average annual temperature is between 15℃ and 22℃. It has a frost-free period of 250 to 330 days a year, and an annual precipitation averaging between 1,400 mm and 2,000 mm, making it one of the provinces with the most rainfall in China.

梅花盛开的福州鼓岭
Fuzhou Guling: Plum blossoms in full bloom

福建野生动植物种类丰富。野生脊椎动物 1733 种，已定名昆虫万余种，高等植物 5550 种，其中国家重点保护野生动物 291 种，国家重点保护野生植物 130 种及变种。福建海洋生物种类 3000 多种，水产品种类占世界之50%，贝、藻、鱼、虾种类数量居全国前列，有闽东、闽中、闽南、闽外和台湾浅滩五大渔场。

福建已发现矿产 123 种，已探明资源量 122 种，矿产资源种类丰富，能源矿产、水气矿产、黑色金属、有色金属、稀土金属、非金属均有分布，水泥标准砂、铸型用砂、叶蜡石等矿产保有资源量居全国前五。

龙岩梅花山红豆杉生态园
Taxus Ecological Park of Mount Meihua in Longyan

武夷山国家公园内国家一级重点保护野生动物——黄腹角雉
Tragopan caboti, a national first-class protected animal in Wuyishan National Park

Fujian is abundant in flora and fauna. It has 1,733 species of wild vertebrates, more than 10,000 species of insects, and 5,550 species of higher plants, including 291 species which are wild animals of national priority protection, and 130 species which are national key protected wild plants. Fujian is also home to more than 3,000 species of marine life. The types of aquatic products found in Fujian account for 50% of the global total, and the amount of shellfish, algae, fish, and shrimp found there is the highest in China. Besides, there are five fisheries in Fujian: the Mindong Fishery, the Minzhong Fishery, the Minnan Fishery, the Minwai Fishery, and the Taiwan Shoal Fishery.

Fujian is rich in mineral resources, namely energy minerals, gas, ferrous and non-ferrous metals, rare earth metals etc.123 types of minerals has been discovered in Fujian,among them 122 have been proven to have reserves. Besides, cement standard sand, sand for casting, pyrophyllite and other mineral resources rank among the top five in China.

人口民族
POPULATION AND DEMOGRAPHY

截至 2022 年末，福建常住人口为 4188 万人，居住在城镇的人口为 2937 万人，占 70.11%；居住在乡村的人口为 1251 万人，占 29.89%。

福建是少数民族散居省份，全省 56 个民族成分齐全。福建是中国畲族人口最多的省份，境内生活的畲族人口达到 37.47 万人，占中国畲族人口的 50.20%；福建也是回族发祥地之一，回族人口 12.86 万人，占全省少数民族人口的 11.47%。

蟳埔女
Xunbu Women

At the end of 2022, the permanent population of Fujian was 41.88 million, with a population of 29.37 million residing in urban areas, accounting for 70.11%; The population living in rural areas is 12.51 million, accounting for 29.89%.

Fujian is home to all of China's 56 ethnic groups. It is the province with the largest population of She ethnic group in China, with a population of 374,700 living within its borders, accounting for 50.20% of China's She population. Fujian is also one of the birthplaces of the Hui ethnic group, with a population of 128600, accounting for 11.47% of the minority population in the province.

惠安女
Hui'an Girls

湄洲女
Meizhou Women

畲族女
Girls of She Nationality

FUJIAN,
A PROVINCE WITH A RICH CULTURAL HISTORY

2

人文福建

历史沿革 ▉▉▊▎▏
HISTORICAL DEVELOPMENT

福建历史悠久，远古属百越之闽越。秦代时置闽中郡，汉代初年（公元前 202 年）立闽越国，汉高祖立无诸为闽越王，都东冶。三国时置建安郡。唐代开元二十一年（733 年）置福建经略使，始称"福建"。北宋置福建路，南宋设"一府五州二军"8 个同级行政机构，于是有了"八闽"之称。明清时置福建布政使司，辛亥革命后置福建省。1949 年 8 月 24 日，成立福建省人民政府。

Fujian has a long history.In ancient times, it was once Minyue, one of the Yue states. During the Qin Dynasty, this region was known as Minzhong Prefecture. During the early Han Dynasty (202 BC), it was Minyue State, ruled by Wuzhu as appointed by Emperor Gaozu of the Han Dynasty, and the capital was Dongye. During the Three Kingdoms Period, it was known as Jian'an Prefecture. In the 21st year (733) of the reign of Emperor Xuanzong of the Tang Dynasty, the post of Fujian military commissioner was formally established, and the region was henceforth known referred to as "Fujian". During the Northern Song Dynasty, it was known as the Fujian Circuit, and included one prefecture, five sub-prefectures, and two military prefectures during the Southern Song Dynasty. For this reason, it was also referred to as the Eight Min (eight administrative divisions). During the Ming and Qing dynasties, an Office of Administrative Commissioner was established in this region. After the 1911 Revolution, this region was named Fujian Province, and the People's Government of Fujian Province was established on August 24, 1949.

| 武夷山汉城遗址
The Hancheng Ruins of Wuyi Mountain

| 昙石山文化遗址
Ruins of Tanshishan Culture

位于福州市闽侯县的昙石山文化遗址距今四五千年，是福建重要的新石器时代遗址，是福建古文明的摇篮、先秦闽族的发祥地。昙石山文化点亮了福建 5000 年的文明之光。

The Tanshishan Cultural Ruins, located in Minhou County, Fuzhou City, is an important Neolithic site in Fujian, which dates back 4000 to 5000 years. It is the cradle of Fujian's ancient civilization and the birthplace of the Min people during the pre-Qin period.The Tanshishan Culture has illuminated the 5000 year old civilization of Fujian.

位于福建三明的万寿岩遗址距今约 18 万年，是中国南方典型的洞穴类型旧石器时代遗址。考古专家们在此发现了世界上罕见的早期人工石铺面、排水沟槽等遗迹。

The Wanshou Rock Paleolithic Site, located in Sanming, Fujian Province, is a typical Paleolithic cave site in southern China, with a history of about 180000 years. Archaeological experts have discovered rare early artifacts such as artificial stone paving and drainage ditches in the world.

三明万寿岩遗址
Wanshou Rock Paleolithic Relics in Sanming

多元文化
DIVERSIFIED CULTURES

　　自晋唐以来，南渐的中原文化与福建本地闽越文化相互融合、相互浸润。至近现代西学东渐，开眼看世界的福建人从不同文明中汲取精华，孕育出异彩纷呈、生机勃勃的地方特色文化。朱子文化、妈祖文化、船政文化、客家文化、闽南文化、海洋文化、侯官文化、红色文化独具魅力，焕发着沉雄葳蕤的生命气象。

　　福建"福"文化绚丽多姿。近年来，福建省积极推动"福"文化传承创新，让文化赋能，"福"文化的内涵与外延在不断丰富，影响力不断扩大。

武夷精舍是朱熹创建的重要书院
Wuyi Academy is an important
academy established by Zhu Xi.

| 三坊七巷水榭戏台
Waterside Stage at the "Three Lanes and Seven Alleys"

Since the Jin and Tang Dynasties, the Central Plains culture had gradually spread to the south and the local Minyue culture in Fujian have integrated and infiltrated each other. In modern times, western learning has spread to the east,Fujian people who have opened their eyes to the world have drawn essence from different civilizations, and bred a colorful and vibrant local cultures, such as Zhuzi Culture, Mazu Culture, Shipping-building Culture, Hakka Culture, Minnan Culture, Ocean Culture, Houguan Culture and Red Culture.

Fujian's "Fu" culture is colorful and diverse. In recent years, Fujian Province has actively promoted the inheritance and innovation of "Fu" culture, enriching the connotation and extension of "Fu" culture, and expanding its influence.

湄洲妈祖祖庙妈祖祭祀大典
A Mazu Sacrificial Ceremony at the Mazu Temple in Meizhou, Putian

1866 年，闽浙总督左宗棠在福州马尾创办了福建船政，沈葆桢为第一任钦差船政大臣

In 1866, Zuo Zongtang, then Viceroy of Fujian and Zhejiang, founded Fujian Shipbuilding Administration in Mawei, Fuzhou. Shen Baozhen was the first imperial shipbuilding minister.

戏剧艺术 ||||

DRAMA

　　福建保留了众多活态戏曲样式，现有 23 个戏曲剧种、4 种木偶戏、1 种皮影戏，其中有 24 项被列入国家级非物质文化遗产名录。福建戏曲剧种历史悠久、声腔多样，除了闽剧、梨园戏、莆仙戏、高甲戏、歌仔戏（芗剧）五大剧种以外，还有京剧、越剧、闽西汉剧、潮剧以及稀有剧种大腔戏、四平戏、打城戏、北路戏等。

（左）闽剧又称福州戏，是现存唯一用福州方言演唱的戏曲剧种。

(Left)Min Opera, also known as Fuzhou Opera, is the only existing opera performed in Fuzhou dialect. The picture shows the 2021 version of Lychee for Crimson Peach.

（右上）梨园戏是福建省的传统戏曲之一。梨园戏发源于宋元时期的泉州，与浙江的南戏并称为"搬演南宋戏文唱念声腔"的"闽浙之音"，被誉为"古南戏活化石"

(Upper right)Liyuan Opera is one of the traditional operas in Fujian Province. Liyuan opera originated in Quanzhou during the Song and Yuan Dynasties. Together with the Southern Opera in Zhejiang Province, Liyuan opera is called "the sound of Fujian and Zhejiang" and is known as the living fossil of ancient Southern Opera".

（右下）莆仙戏源于唐、成于宋、盛于明清，用兴化方言演唱，具有浓厚的地方色彩

(Upper left)Puxian Opera originated in the Tang Dynasty, developed in the Song Dynasty, and flourished in the Ming and Qing Dynasties. It is performed in the Xinghua dialect, with strong local characteristics.

（左）高甲戏发祥地为福建泉州，最初源于明末清初闽南农村流行的一种装扮梁山英雄、表演武打技术的化装游行，是闽南诸剧种中流播区域最广、观众面最多的一个地方戏曲剧种

(Left)The birthplace of Gaojia Opera is Quanzhou, Fujian Province. It originated from a popular costume parade which dressed as Liangshan heroes and performed martial arts skills in the rural area of southern Fujian in the late Ming and early Qing dynasties.It is the most widely spread and widely watched local opera among the southern Fujian operas.

Fujian has dynamically preserved a number of operas. At present, there are 23 types of opera, four types of puppet shows, and one type of shadow puppetry, 24 of which have been included in China's list of national intangible cultural heritage. Fujian operas, which have a long history, feature a variety of operatic tunes. In addition to the Min Opera, Liyuan Opera, Puxian Opera, Gaojia Opera, Hokkien Opera (Xiang Opera), there are also Peking Opera, Yue Opera, Han Opera of Western Fujian, Teochew Opera, and rare operas such as Daqiang Opera, Siping Opera, Dacheng Opera, and Beilu Opera.

（中）芗剧原名歌仔戏，是流行于福建漳州芗江一带的汉族戏曲剧种

(Middle)Xiang Opera, formerly known as Gezi Opera, is a kind of Han Opera popular in Xiangjiang area of Zhangzhou, Fujian Province.

（右）泉州提线木偶戏是福建省的传统戏剧，至今保存七百余出传统剧目和由三百余支曲牌唱腔构成的独特剧种音乐"傀儡调"

(Right)Quanzhou's string puppetry is a traditional drama in Fujian Province, which has preserved over 700 traditional repertoires and a unique musical form called "puppet tune" composed of over 300 qupai vocals.

匠心巧作 ||
ARTS AND CRAFTS

福建是中国传统工艺美术四大重点产区之一，有雕塑（包括石雕、木雕、玉雕等）、漆艺、陶瓷、工艺花画、竹草藤编织、金属工艺品等 13 大类 100 多个品种，既有精湛的收藏型艺术精品，也有大众化的实用工艺品。其中，福州寿山石雕、脱胎漆器、软木画、厦门漆线雕、莆田木雕、仙游古典家具、德化工艺陶瓷、惠安石雕等，不仅技艺精湛、风格独特、久负盛名，而且产业规模不断扩大。福建陶瓷是中国古代海上丝绸之路的重要货物之一，与丝绸、茶一起远涉重洋。

福州寿山石
Fuzhou Shoushan Stone seals

德化瓷雕作品《贵妃醉酒》
Dehua porcelain carving Drunkened Concubine

Fujian is one of the four key production areas of traditional Chinese arts and crafts,with more than 100 varieties in 13 categories, including carvings (e.g., stone carvings, wood carvings, jade carvings, etc.), lacquerware art, art ceramics, handicraft flower painting, bamboo, straw and vine weaving, and metal handicrafts. The products range from exquisite works for professional collectors to practical handicrafts. Among them,Fuzhou Shoushan stone carvings, bodiless lacquerware, cork paintings, Xiamen lacquer line carvings, Putian wood carvings, Xianyou classical furniture, Dehua ceramics, and Hui'an stone carvings are exquisite in skill and distinctive in style. Besides, the industry is expanding.Fujian ceramics is one of the important goods on the Maritime Silk Road in ancient China, and it has traveled across the oceans together with silk and tea.

| 惠安石雕
Hui'an Stone Carving

莆田木雕《百鸟朝凤》
Putian Wood Carving *Birds Paying Homage to the Phoenix*

丝路茶香 |

MIN TEA TRAVELING ACROSS THE SILK ROAD

福建产茶历史悠久。东晋太元丙子年的"莲花茶襟"比陆羽《茶经》早300多年。得天独厚的自然条件，山川之秀灵、物种之丰富，造就了福建茶类多样、品种争奇。宋元两朝斗茶兴盛，蔚然成风。明清开创红茶、乌龙茶、白茶、茉莉花茶制茶工艺。17世纪初武夷茶开始外销，风靡欧洲。如今，安溪铁观音、武夷岩茶、福鼎白茶、正山小种、福州茉莉花茶、坦洋工夫、漳平水仙等名茶享誉海内外。

| 高山茶园
Scene of a High-Mountain Tea Garden

| 宋建窑酱黄釉盏
Black Glazed Tea Cup Produced by Jian
of the Song Dynasty

Tea production has a long history in Fujian. Lianhua Chajin, inscribed in 376 on a stone, predated Lu Yu's "Classic of Tea" by more than 300 years. The unique natural conditions, picturesque mountains and rivers, and abundance species have created a variety of tea varieties in Fujian. Furthermore, tea competitions were common during the Song and Yuan Dynasties. During the Ming and Qing Dynasties, the processing techniques of black tea, oolong tea, white tea, and jasmine tea were developed. In the early 17th century, Wuyi tea began to be exported and became popular in Europe. Today, Anxi Tieguanyin, Wuyi Rock Tea, Fuding White Tea, Lapsang Souchong, Fuzhou Jasmine Tea, Tanyang Gongfu tea and Zhangping Shuixian tea enjoy great popularity in China and around the world.

| 武夷山大红袍
Dahongpao Tea Trees on Mount Wuyi

茉莉花茶是将茶叶和茉莉花进行拼合、窨制，使茶叶吸收花香而成
Jasmine tea is made by combining tea leaves and Jasmine petals and scenting them, allowing the tea leaves to absorb the fragrance of the flowers.

世界遗产

福建省世界遗产丰厚，有武夷山世界文化与自然双遗产，有福建土楼、鼓浪屿：历史
国际社区、泉州：宋元中国的世界海洋商贸中心等世界文化遗产和中国丹霞泰宁世界自然
遗产。有莆田木兰陂、黄鞠灌溉工程、福清天宝陂等世界灌溉工程遗产。全省共有 9 个项
目入选联合国教科文组织非遗名录（名册），是我国迄今在联合国教科文组织非遗保护三
个系列上获得大满贯的唯一省份，其中南音、妈祖信俗、中国剪纸（漳浦、柘荣）、中国
传统木结构营造技艺（闽南民居）、送王船——有关人与海洋可持续联系的仪式及相关实
践、中国传统制茶技艺及其相关习俗 6 个项目入选人类非物质文化遗产代表作名录，中国
木拱桥传统营造技艺、中国水密隔舱福船制造技艺 2 个项目入选急需保护的非物质文化遗
产名录，《福建木偶戏传承人培养计划》入选优秀实践名册。

世界自然与文化双遗产——武夷山
World Natural and Cultural Heritage Mount Wuyi

永定客家土楼承启楼闹元宵
Celebration of the Lantern Festival in Chengqi Dwelling, Hakka Tulou
(a building complex of Hakka people) in Yongding

Fujian Province abounds in world heritages, including Mount Wuyi World Cultural and Natural Heritage, the Earthen Building in Fujian Province, Gulangyu: Historical International Community, Quanzhou: World Marine Trade Center of China in the Song and Yuan Dynasties, and China Danxia Taining World Natural Heritage. There are world irrigation engineering heritage sites such as Mulanbei in Putian, Huangju Irrigation Project in Ningde and Tianbaobei in Fuqing. It is the only province in China with a total of nine projects selected for the UNESCO's Intangible Cultural Heritage protection series so far.The Representative List of the Intangible Cultural Heritage of Humanity includes six items: Nanyin, Mazu Belief in Customs, Chinese Paper Cuttings (Zhangpu, Zherong), Chinese traditional wood structure building skills (Minnan folk houses), sending royal boats-a ceremony, rituals, and related practices to maintain the sustainable connection between humans and the sea, and Chinese traditional tea processing techniques and related customs.Two projects, the traditional construction techniques of Chinese wooden arch bridges and the manufacturing techniques of Chinese watertight compartments and lucky boats, were selected for the list of intangible cultural heritage that urgently needs protection. The "Fujian Puppet Show Inheritor Training Plan" was selected for the list of excellent practices.

"泉州：宋元中国的世界海洋商贸中心"于 2021 年被列入世界文化遗产。图为远眺泉州东西塔
Quanzhou: World Marine Trade Center of China in the Song and Yuan Dynasties was listed as a World Cultural Heritage in 2021. The picture shows a distant view of the East West Pagoda in Quanzhou

（上）2017 年，"鼓浪屿：历史国际社区"成为世界文化遗产
(Upper) "Kulangsu, a Historic International Settlement" was included in the World Cultural Heritage List in 2017

（下）泉州南安蔡氏古民居建筑群
(Lower)Ancient Residential Buildings of the Cai's Family in Nan'an, Quanzhou

寿宁杨梅州桥
Yangmeizhou Bridge,
Shouning

漳州港尾送王船
Sending a Royal Boat in Zhangzhou Port

柘荣剪纸
Zherong Paper-cuttings

泉州南音——历史悠久的古老乐种，被誉为"中国音乐史上的活化石"
Quanzhou Nanyin — An Ancient Music Honored as the "Living Fossil in the History of Chinese Music"

FUJIAN,
A PROSPEROUS
AND STRONG PROVINCE

新项目成果交易会

3

富强福建

科技创新
SCIENTIFIC AND TECHNOLOGICAL INNOVATION

　　福建坚持"创新型省份"建设一张蓝图绘到底，以科技创新催生新发展动能。

　　福厦泉国家自主创新示范区和国家创新型省份获批建设、21 世纪海上丝绸之路核心区创新发展试验获得支持。2022 年福建全社会研发投入年均增长 15%，比全国平均水平高 4.6 个百分点。国家高新技术企业总数增长两倍多。每万人口发明专利拥有量和技术市场合同交易额翻一番多。福州、厦门、泉州、龙岩进入国家创新型城市行列，晋江、福清进入国家创新型县（市）行列。高新技术产业化效益指数居全国第 4 位，科技促经济社会发展指数居全国第 9 位，科技创新环境指数居全国第 9 位，公民具备科学素质比例居全国第 7 位。

福州高新区
Fuzhou High-tech Industrial Development Zone

华为晋江工业互联网孵化中心
Huawei (Jinjiang) Industrial Internet Incubation Center

Fujian adheres to the blueprint for developing itself into an innovation-driven province and employs scientific and technological innovation to generate new growth drivers.

The construction of national independent innovation demonstration zones in Fuzhou, Xiamen, and Quanzhou, the construction of the national innovation-oriented province, and the pilot program in the core area of innovation and development of the 21st Century Maritime Silk Road all received approval and support. In 2022, the average annual growth rate of Fujian's R&D investment was 15%, which was 4.6

中国·海峡创新项目成果交易会
China Straits Innovation and Projects Fair

percentage points higher than the national average; the total number of national high-tech enterprises has more than doubled; the number of invention patents per 10,000 people and the trading volume of technical contracts have more than doubled; Fuzhou, Xiamen, Quanzhou, Longyan, Jinjiang and Fuqing have joined the ranks of national innovation-driven cities and counties. Additionally, the efficiency index of high-tech industrialization ranked fourth, the index for economic and social development promoted ranked ninth, the index for the scientific and technological innovation environment ranked ninth, and the proportion of residents with scientific literacy ranked seventh nationally.

产业发展

福建推进产业结构持续优化升级，初步形成了以先进制造业和现代服务业为主体、特色现代农业为基础的现代产业体系。目前，福建培育了 67 家百亿工业企业，21 个千亿产业集群，其中，电子信息、先进装备制造、石油化工、现代纺织服装产业已经达到万亿级。国家高新技术企业突破 1 万家，新增国家专精特新"小巨人"企业 132 家。2022 年，福建实现地区生产总值 5.3 万亿元，比上年增长 4.7%。民营企业是福建发展活力的重要源泉，民营经济占全省经济总量近七成。

福建正布局战略性新兴产业七大重点领域，新一代信息技术、高端装备、新材料、新能源、生物与新医药、节能环保、海洋高新等，将成为引领福建未来产业发展的重要力量。

上汽集团宁德生产基地
Ningde Shanghai Automobile Production Base

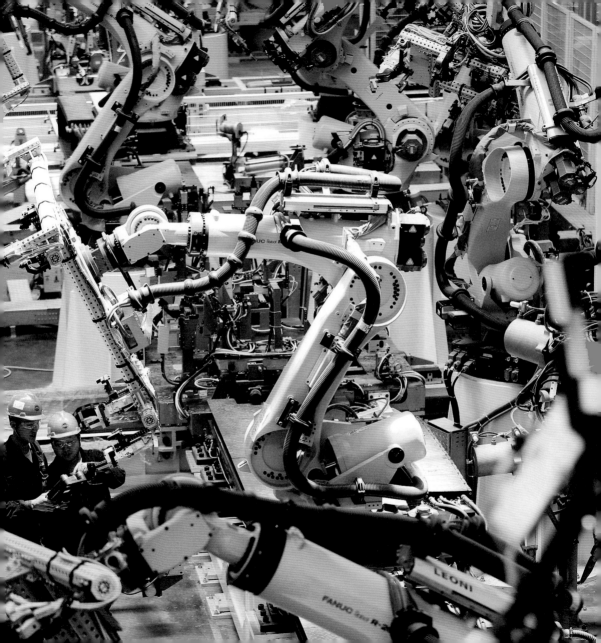

福建福耀玻璃是全球规模最大的汽车玻璃供应商，全球每 4 块汽车玻璃就有一块来自福耀（人民日报 供图）

Fujian Fuyao Glass is the world's largest automotive glass supplier. One out of every four pieces of automotive glass in the world comes from Fuyao. (Photo provided by People's Daily)

Fujian is continuously optimizing and upgrading its industrial structure, and has preliminary established a modern industrial system that focuses on advanced manufacturing and modern service industries and is rooted in modern agriculture with Chinese characteristics. At present, Fujian has cultivated 67 industrial enterprises, with each valuing RMB 10 billion, and 21 industrial clusters, with each valuing RMB 100 billion, including electronic information, advanced equipment manufacturing, petrochemical engineering, and modern textile and clothing industries, with each valuing RMB one trillion. The number of national high-tech enterprises has exceeded 10000, and 132 new national specialized, refined, and new "little giant" enterprises have been added.In 2022, Fujian's regional gross production reached RMB 5.3 trillion, an increase of 4.7% over the previous year. Private enterprises are an important source of vitality for Fujian's economic development, accounting for nearly 70% of the province's economic aggregate.

Fujian is laying out seven key areas of strategic emerging industries. The province's future industrial development will be driven by new-generation information technology, high-end equipment, new materials, new energy, biology and new medicine, energy conservation and environmental protection, and marine high-tech.

数字经济
DIGITAL ECONOMY

　　国家主席习近平曾在福建工作期间，作出了建设"数字福建"的战略部署，开启了福建推进信息化建设的进程。数字福建是数字中国的思想源头和实践起点。

　　福建始终把数字福建作为高质量发展的基础性先导性工程，持续推进数字化发展，以信息化培育新动能，用新动能推动新发展，以新发展创造新辉煌。2022年，福建省加快实施做大做强做优数字经济行动，进一步发挥数字中国建设峰会平台效应，积极借助国家数字经济创新发展试验区、公共数据资源开发利用等国家级试点政策带来的溢出效应，不断激活数字生态，全省数字基础设施更加夯实，数字经济核心产业加快壮大，产业数字化转型持续深化，公共数据资源化价值化稳步推进，数字化公共服务能力全面提升，全年数字经济增加值预计突破2.6万亿元，为福建高质量发展注入强劲动能。

　　2023年第六届数字中国建设峰会
　　The 6th Digital China Summit in 2023

福州长乐数字小镇
Changle Digital Town, Fuzhou

During his work in Fujian, Xi Jinping, President of China, made the strategic decision to build a digital Fujian, initiating the process of promoting information-based construction in Fujian. Digital Fujian is the ideological origin and starting point for the construction of Digital China.

Fujian has always regarded digital Fujian as the most important and leading project for high-quality development. It continues to promote digital development, foster new growth drivers through informatization, and promote new developments with new growth drivers in order to create new brilliance. In 2022, Fujian Province accelerated the implementation of the action plan to make the digital economy bigger, stronger, and better, continued to give full play to the Digital China Summit's role as a platform, and continued to activate the digital ecology by leveraging the spillover effects of national pilot program policies such as national pilot zones for the innovative development of the digital economy and pilot zones for the development and use of public data resources. Fujian has further strengthened its digital infrastructure, accelerated the expansion of core industries of the digital economy, further deepened the industrial digital transformation, steadily promoted the resource and value application of public data, and comprehensively improved the capacity of digital public services. It is estimated that the annual value added of the digital economy will exceed RMB 2.6 trillion, adding strong momentum to the province's quality development.

海洋经济 II
MARINE ECONOMY

作为海洋资源大省，福建"渔、港、景、能"资源丰富，发展海洋经济空间潜力巨大。2021年，福建省出台《"十四五"海洋强省建设专项规划》《加快建设"海上福建"推进海洋经济高质量发展三年行动方案（2021-2023）》，推进海岛、海岸带、海洋"点线面"综合开发。"一带两核六湾多岛"的区域海洋经济发展格局逐步形成，海洋旅游业、海洋渔业、海洋交通运输业三大海洋优势产业不断壮大。建设福州、厦门国家海洋经济发展示范区，建成百余个国家级、省部级涉海科技创新平台、海洋种业、海洋碳汇、海洋生物医药等关键技术攻关取得突破。

2022年，福建省海洋生产总值约1.2万亿元，占地区生产总值23%，继续保持全国前列；全省水产品总量862万吨，居全国第三；水产品出口额85亿美元，连续十年居全国首位；渔民人均纯收入2.75万元，同比增长6.6%，继续保持全国前列。

| 宁德霞浦海上养殖
Xiapu marine aquaculture, Ningde

As a large province with abundant marine resources, Fujian has a great number of fisheries, harbors, landscape, and energy resources, and has great potential for the development of the marine economy. In 2021, Fujian provincial government issued the Special Plan for Building a Strong Marine Province in the 14th Five-Year Plan Period and the Three-year Action Plan for Accelerating the Building of "Marine Fujian" and Promoting Quality Development of Marine Economy (2021-2023) to promote the integrated development of islands, coastal zones, and oceans. The regional marine economy development pattern of "one zone, two core areas, six bays, and multiple islands" has gradually taken shape, and three advantageous marine industries, that is, marine tourism, marine fishery, and marine transportation, are growing. Furthermore, national demonstration zones for marine economy development have been established in Fuzhou and Xiamen, and more than 100 national,

provincial, and ministerial platforms for innovation in marine science and technology have been developed, leading to breakthroughs in key technologies, including marine seed industry, marine carbon sink, and marine bio-medicine.

In 2022, Fujian's gross marine production was estimated at RMB 1.2 trillion, accounting for 23% of the regional gross production and remaining the country's top performer; the total amount of aquatic products in the province was 8.62 million tons, ranking third in China; the export of aquatic products reached USD 8.5 billion, ranking first in China for ten consecutive years;the per capita net income of fishermen was RMB 27,500, up 6.6% year on year, remaining the country's top performer.

| 位于湄洲湾北岸经济开发区的国投配煤基地
SDIC Coal Blending Base in North Coast Economic Development Zone, Meizhou Bay

福建是中国南方地区重要的生态屏障，森林覆盖率 65.12%，是中国最绿省份。福建是中国首个省级生态文明先行示范区、中国首个国家生态文明试验区。

福建持续深化生态省建设，努力建好国家生态文明试验区，以占全国约 1.3% 的土地、2.9% 的能源消费创造全国约 4.4% 的经济总量。木兰溪治理、生态保护补偿等 39 项改革举措和经验做法向

龙岩长汀湿地公园
Changting Wetland Park in Longyan

全国复制推广，河湖长制、林长制全面推行，生态文明指数全国第一。福建将"双碳"战略目标纳入生态省布局，坚定不移走生态优先、绿色低碳的高质量发展道路，始终坚持生产绿色化、生态产业化、能源清洁化、生活低碳化。不断加快传统产业生态化转型，生态产业链加速形成，能源结构、城乡建设、消费方式全面"绿化"。全省因绿而美，向绿而强，绿色经济正成为福建发展的新增长极。

With a forest coverage rate of 65.12%, Fujian is an important ecological barrier in southern China and the greenest province in China. It is the first provincial and national ecological civilization pilot zone in China.

Fujian continues to strengthen the construction of an ecological province and strives to build a national pilot zone for ecological civilization. With about 1.3% of the country's land and 22.9% of its energy consumption, Fujian contributes about 4.4% of the country's gross domestic product (GDP). A total of 39 reform measures and practices of Fujian, including the Mulan River governance and ecological protection compensation, have been adopted and promoted nationwide. The river and lake chief system and the forest chief system have been fully implemented, with its ecological civilization index ranked first in China. Fujian also incorporates the "Dual Carbon" Policy into the plan to build an ecological province. Besides, it continues to accelerate the ecological transformation of traditional industries and the formation of an ecological industrial chain to create a more environmental friendly energy structure, urban and rural construction, and consumption patterns. The green economy is emerging as a new growth engine for the development of Fujian.

武夷山国家公园
Wuyishan National Park

文旅经济

CULTURAL AND TOURISM ECONOMY

　　福建山海资源丰富，自然风光秀美，地域文化独特，素有"山海画廊、人间福地"美誉，发展文旅经济的条件得天独厚。

　　2022年，福建省印发《福建省推进文旅经济高质量发展行动计划（2022—2025年）》，推出"十大行动"，进一步做好"山海文章"。以全线1160公里的武夷山国家公园森林步道为串联，依托全省海岸线长度全国第2位、海岸线曲折率全国第1位的优势，高标准打造1号滨海风景道。发展红色、生态、工业、乡村、海洋、康养等文旅新业态，丰富全域生态旅游产品供给，打造平潭国际旅游岛，打响"清新福建""福文化"等品牌，建设文化强省和全域生态旅游省。

| 泉州洛阳古街"古风市集"吸引众多游客
The ancient-style market of Luoyang Ancient Street in Quanzhou attracts lots of tourists

福州鼓岭柱里露营地，打造年轻人向往的自然社区
Kuliang Zhuli Campsite in Fuzhou, a natural community that young people yearn for

With abundant mountain and marine resources, beautiful natural scenery, and distinct regional culture, Fujian is a picturesque and great place that offers unique conditions for the development of a cultural and tourism economy.

In 2022, Fujian provincial government issued the Action Plan of Fujian Province for Promoting High-quality Development of Cultural and Tourism Economy (2022-2025), and enacted ten measures to advance and utilize mountain and marine resources. Fujian has built, the best coastal scenic roads, which connects with the 1,160-kilometer forest trail in Wuyishan National Park, and draws on the advantages of China's second-longest coastline with the highest curvature rate. The province has also developed new business forms of cultural tourism, including the red revolution, ecology, industry, rural areas, marine, and healthcare, enriched the supply of ecological tourism products across the entire region, constructed the Pingtan International Tourism Island, and promoted associated brands such as the "Fresh Fujian" and "Fu Culture".

东山岛环岛路
The Ring Road of Dongshan Island

FUJIAN,
A HAPPY PROVINCE

4

幸福福建

教育塑才
EDUCATION

　　教育是事关社会发展和民生福祉的国之大计，福建坚持教育优先发展战略。2021年，福建省人民政府与国家教育部签订战略合作协议，部省共同推进福建教育高质量发展。2021年全省教育经费投入达1600.28亿元、年均增长8.3%，在全国率先实现义务教育发展基本均衡县全覆盖。

　　全省现有各级各类学校1.58万所，在校学生925.1万人，教职工72万人，学前教育三年入园率99.1%；九年义务教育巩固率保持在99%以上；高中阶段毛入学率97.42%；高等教育毛入学率61.61%。福建教育体系不断完善，基本满足人民群众"有学上"需求，向"上好学"目标迈进。

厦门大学
Xiamen University

Education is of great importance for China's social development and people's well-being. Fujian adheres to the strategy of prioritizing educational development, and has signed a strategic cooperation agreement with the Ministry of Education to jointly promote the high-quality development of education in Fujian in 2021. In the same year, Fujian invested RMB 160.028 billion in education, an average annual increase of 8.3%, making it the first province in China to implement balanced development of compulsory education in all its counties.

There are now 15,800 schools of all levels and types, with 9.251 million students and 720,000 faculty members. The three-year enrollment rate of preschool education is 99.1, while the retention rate of nine-year compulsory education remains above 99%. The gross enrollment rate of high schools is 97.42%, while the gross enrollment rate of higher education is 61.61%. Fujian has continued to improve its education system to meet people's needs for "having access to education", making progress toward the goal of "having access to good education".

福州市铜盘中心小学的非遗课程"福州油纸伞"
The intangible cultural heritage course "Oil-paper Umbrellas of Fuzhou" in Tongpan Central Primary School, Fuzhou

第四届中国互联网＋大学生创新创业大赛在厦门大学举行
The Fourth China College Students' 'Internet Plus' Innovation and Entrepreneurship Competition was held at Xiamen University.

社保惠民

SOCIAL SECURITY SYSTEM BENEFITING THE PEOPLE

　　福建不断健全多层次的社会保障体系。企业职工基本养老保险全国统筹稳步实施，失业保险、工伤保险省级统筹加快推进，社会保障待遇水平稳步提高，基金安全持续加强。

　　截至 2023 年 2 月，全省城镇职工基本养老保险参保人数（含离退休）为 1701.86 万人，城乡居民基本养老保险参保人数 1595.79 万人，参加基本医疗保险人数，全省工伤保险参保人数为 1010.96 万人，全省失业保险参保人数为 746.82 万人。

Fujian has continued to improve the multi-level social security system by consistently implementing nationwide consolidation of basic pension insurance for enterprise employees, accelerating the provincial consolidation of unemployment insurance and occupational injury insurance, steadily improving the level of social security benefits, and continuously enhancing fund security.

As of February 2023, 17.0186 million people were covered by basic pension insurance for urban workers (including retirees), 15.9579 million by basic pension old-age insurance for urban and rural residents, 10.1096 million by basic medical insurance and occupational injury insurance, and 7.4682 million by unemployment insurance.

加强社会保障体系建设。福建省税务系统将社保费纲入税收一体管理
Fujian Provincial Taxa System incorporated social insurance premium into integrated taxation management to strengthen the development of social security system.

国家紧急医学救援队（福建）
National Emergency Medical Rescue Team (Fujian)

福建在深化医药卫生体制改革，促进医保、医疗、医药协同发展，全面推进健康福建建设方面持续发力。

推进公立医院高质量发展，加快国家和省级区域医疗中心项目、医疗"创双高"等建设，打造区域医疗高地。夯实基层医疗服务网底，强化县域、乡村医疗卫生资源统筹。提升各类医联（共）体运行效益，为群众提供同质化、连续性、高效率医疗服务。

2022年末，共有各级各类医疗卫生机构2.91万个，7个国家区域医疗中心项目落地实施，首批4个省级区域医疗中心项目布局建设；公立医院综合改革效果评价连续7年位居全国前列；共建成居家社区养老服务照料中心662所，实现街道和中心城区乡镇100%覆盖。全省医养结合机构发展至184家，医养结合床位4.92万张。人均预期寿命提高至78.85岁，居民主要健康指标保持全国前列。

Fujian remains committed to advancing medical and healthcare system reform, encouraging the coordinated development of medical insurance, medical care, and medicine, and comprehensively promoting the construction of a healthy Fujian.

Fujian has actively promoted the quality development of public hospitals and accelerated the construction of national and provincial-level regional medical center projects, as well as high-level hospitals and clinical medical centers, to establish a regional medical plateau. Fujian has also consolidated the basic medical service network, strengthened the coordination of medical and healthcare resources at the county and village levels, and improved the operational efficiency of various medical associations (service communities) to provide homogeneous, continuous, and effective medical services to the people.

As of the end of 2022, Fujian has a total of 29,100 medical and healthcare institutions of various levels and types, implemented seven national regional medical center projects, and completed the design and construction of the first batch of four provincial-level regional medical center projects. It also has a comprehensive evaluation of the reform effect on public hospitals that have ranked first in China for seven consecutive years. Besides, a total of 662 home-based community elderly care centers were built, achieving full coverage of streets and towns in central urban areas. There were also 184 institutions providing integrated medical and elderly care services, with 49,200 beds. As a result, the average life expectancy in Fujian has increased to 78.85 years, and the main health indicators of residents remain at the forefront of the country.

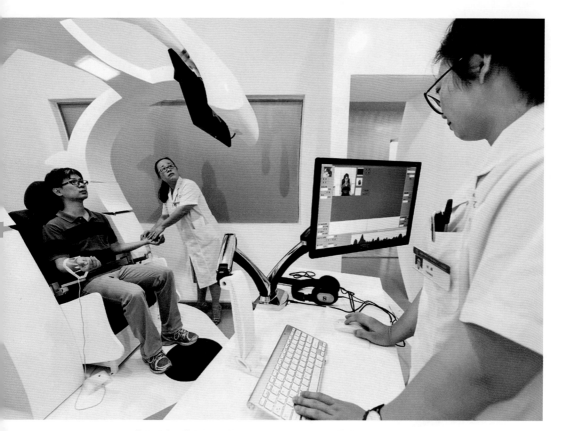

福建中医药大学附属第三人民医院，"中医健康管理太空舱"可为市民做全套中医健康体检
The "TCM Health Management Capsule" at the Third People's Hospital Fujian University of Traditional Chinese Medicine can provide citizens with a complete set of TCM health examinations.

福州海峡奥林匹克体育中心，是全省规模最大的体育主题公园
Fuzhou Strait Olympic Sports Center is the largest sports theme park in the province.

| "福文化"主题书店
Fu Culture themed bookstore

| 第 33 届中国电影金鸡奖在厦门举行
The 33rd Golden Rooster Awards was held in Xiamen.

福建积极推进全民健身场地设施建设，县、乡、村三级公共健身设施和社区 15 分钟健身圈基本覆盖，健身步道总长突破一万千米。城区"15 分钟健身圈"基本建成，行政村全民健身场地设施全覆盖，全省人均体育场地面积达 2.57 平方米。

福建已基本建成覆盖城乡、便捷高效、保基本、促公平的现代公共文化服务体系。共有国有艺术表演团体 70 个、公共图书馆 95 个、文化馆 95 个、博物馆 147 家、档案馆 125 家、影院 395 家，全年出版图书 5157 种。2022 年，泉州成为福建继厦门、三明、福州之后第 4 个获评国家公共文化服务体系示范区的地市。南平市文化艺术馆、鼓楼区文化馆入选全国公共文化云基层智能服务端 2022 年首批典型应用案例。福建公共文化服务不断"出圈"。

Fujian actively promotes the construction of national fitness facilities, with basic coverage of county-level, township, and village level public fitness facilities and community 15 minute fitness circles. The total length of fitness trails has exceeded 10000 kilometers. The "15 minute fitness circle" in the urban area has been basically completed, and the administrative villages have fully covered the facilities of national fitness venues. The per capita sports area in the province reaches 2.57 square meters.

Fujian has substantially established a modern public cultural service system that covers both urban and rural areas, is convenient and efficient, ensures basic services, and promotes fairness. There are a total of 70 state-owned art performance troupes, 95 public libraries, 95 cultural centers, 147 museums, 125 archives, and 395 cinemas, and 5,157 books are published throughout the year. In 2022, Quanzhou became the fourth city in Fujian to be awarded the National Public Cultural Service System Demonstration Zone, after Xiamen, Sanming, and Fuzhou. In the same year, Nanping Cultural and Art Center and Gulou District Cultural Center were selected as the first batch of typical application cases of the national public cultural cloud grassroots intelligent server, further expanding the influence of Fujian's public cultural services.

福州金牛山福道
Fudao on Jinniu Mountain, Fuzhou

闽菜，是中国八大菜系之一；闽味小吃，走出福建，闻名全国。闽菜不仅是海内外福建乡亲的舌尖乡愁，同时也是富民强省的特色产业。为进一步推进闽菜繁荣发展，福建于 2021 年 6 月出台促进闽菜繁荣三年行动方案。通过对闽菜技艺文化进行保护，开展八闽美食嘉年华、沙县小吃华夏行系列活动，创建闽菜馆公共品牌等，让八闽美味不断飘扬。

2023 年 3 月，福州举行了第十六届中国餐饮产业发展大会，筹建了第一个以闽菜为主题的博物馆，并积极申创"世界美食之都"。

闽菜汤菜代表——
鸡汤氽海蚌
Boiled Sea Clam in
Chicken Soup, the
representative of
soups in Fujian Cuisine

闽菜招牌"佛跳墙"
"Fotiaoqiang" (Steamed Abalone with Shark's Fin and Fish Maw), one of the most famous dishes in Fujian Cuisine

Fujian cuisine is one of the eight major cuisines in China. In particular, Min style snacks are famous across the country. Fujian cuisine represents the taste of the Fujian people at home and abroad and serves as a characteristic industry to enrich people and strengthen the province. To further promote the development of Fujian cuisine, the Fujian provincial government issued a three-year action plan to promote the prosperity of Fujian cuisine in June 2021. By protecting the arts and culture of Fujian cuisine, holding a series of activities, including the Bamin Food Carnival and China Tour of Shaxian Snacks, and establishing public brands such as Fujian Cuisine Restaurant, Fujian has successfully spread the influence of Fujian cuisine.

In March 2023, Fuzhou held the 16th China Catering Industry Development Conference, opened the first museum with the theme of Fujian cuisine, and actively apply for the title "City of Gastronomy of the World".

宜居宜业

AN ENVIRONMENT SUITABLE FOR RESIDENCE AND CAREER

福建深入实施城市更新行动和乡村建设行动，不断提升城乡基础设施品质，打造宜居宜业的城乡环境。城市更新行动滚动实施，数字城市建设加快推进，全省城镇化率达70.1%，城市更加宜居、更有韧性、更显智慧。乡村振兴战略深入推进，完善乡村治理体系，建设乡村文化设施，整治农村人居环境，美丽乡村成为八闽大地闪亮的明珠。坚持区域协调发展，完善发达地区对相对不发达地区结对帮扶机制，东西部协作和对口支援工作持续深化，构建优势互补、高质量发展的区域经济布局。

2022年全省实施城乡建设品质提升项目7239个，投资5129亿元。宜居宜业，相辅相成。不断完善的"宜居"功能，成为百姓安居乐业的最强基数，人民群众的获得感与幸福感与日俱增。

"上下杭"是福州昔日以商业繁华而闻名的古老街区
"Shanghang and Xiahang" are old city blocks of Fuzhou famous for commercial prosperity in the past.

Fujian has carried out extensive urban renewal and rural construction initiatives to improve the quality of urban and rural infrastructure and create an environment suitable for residence and career continuously engaged in urban renewal measures, and accelerated the construction of digital cities. The entire province has an urbanization rate of up to 70.1%, making its cities more livable, resilient, and smart. Fujian has further advanced the rural revitalization strategy, enhanced the rural governance system, built rural cultural facilities, and improved the rural living environment. Fujian has always adhered to regionally coordinated development, improved the mechanism of paired assistance between developed regions and less-developed regions, further deepened cooperation and paired assistance between the eastern and western regions, and built a regional economic pattern featuring complementary advantages and quality development.

In 2022, with an investment of RMB 512.9 billion, Fujian has implemented 7,239 projects suitable for residence and career , which improves the quality of urban and rural development. The efforts in creating a better environment for residents have become the strongest foundation for people to live and work in peace and contentment, and to increase their sense of gain and happiness.

宁德下党乡打造红色文化、廊桥文化综合性旅游区，成为乡村游的热门打卡地
Integrated Tourism Zone of Red Culture and Corridor Bridge Culture at Xiadang Xiang, Ningde City has become a must-visit tourist attraction in a countryside tour.

FUJIAN,
AN OPEN PROVINCE

5

开放福建

四海联通
TRANSPORTATION

　　福建交通"由通向畅、由畅向优"，全面建成"两纵三横"综合运输通道，在全国率先实现市通高铁、县通高速、镇通干线、村通客车，综合交通发展总体水平迈进全国先进行列。

　　福建全省高速公路通车里程 6156 千米，路网密度居全国前列，81.1% 陆域乡镇实现 30 分钟内上高速。铁路营业里程 4230 千米，中欧（厦门）班列从东南沿海通达亚欧 12 个国家 30 多座城市，实现了与丝绸之路经济带的无缝衔接。所有设区市均建有便捷换乘的综合客运枢纽，所有机场、动车站、客运码头 100% 配套公路客运场站，中心城区实现公交站 500 米全覆盖。福州、厦门迈进"地铁时代"，武夷新区开通了轻轨交通，全省新能源公交车占比 85.8%。

　　福建现有福州长乐国际机场、厦门高崎国际机场、南平武夷山机场、泉州晋江机场、龙岩冠豸山机场、三明沙县机场，境内外航线超 300 条。现代化东南沿海港口群强势崛起，港口吞吐量超过 7 亿吨，拥有 3 个亿吨港。沿海建有生产性泊位 457 个，可停靠世界最大集装箱船、油轮、邮轮和散货船。全省开通集装箱航线约 300 条，通达 50 多个国家和地区的 140 多个主要港口，其中"丝路海运"命名航线达 100 条，联盟成员超 300 家。

Fujian has built a comprehensive transportation network consisting of "two vertical lines and three horizontal lines", and was the first province in China to realize that all cities are connected by high-speed rail, all counties are connected by expressways, every township has access to main roads, and buses pass through every village. Its transportation system ranks among the forefront of the country in terms of overall development.

The length of expressways open to traffic across the province reaches 6,156 kilometers, and the density of its expressway network is among the top in China. In 81.1% of towns and villages, expressways are accessible within 30 minutes. The operating mileage of the railway is 4,230 kilometers, and the China-Europe (Xiamen) Railway Express connects over 30 cities in 12 countries in Asia and Europe from the southeastern Chinese coast, realizing a seamless connection with the Silk Road Economic Belt. All districts have comprehensive passenger transportation hubs with convenient transfers, and all airports, railway stations, and passenger terminals are 100% equipped with highway passenger stations. There are also bus stops every 500 meters in the urban areas, and 85.8% of the province's buses are powered by new energy. Furthermore, subways are available in Fuzhou and Xiamen, while light rail transit services are available in Wuyi New District.

With over 300 domestic and international routes, Fujian Changle International Airport, Xiamen Gaoqi International Airport, Nanping Wuyishan Airport, Quanzhou Jinjiang Airport, Longyan Guanzhishan Airport, and Sanming Shaxian Airport. The modern port group along the southeastern coast is also expanding rapidly, with a port throughput of over 700 million tons and three hundred million ton ports. Along the coast of Fujian, there are 457 productive berths which can accommodate the world's largest container ships, oil tankers, cruise liners, and bulk carriers. Fujian also has about 300 container routes connecting more than 140 major ports in more than 50 countries and regions, Among them, there are 100 named "Silk Road Maritime" routes and over 300 alliance members.

中国首个智慧港口——厦门远海码头
Xiamen Ocean Gate Terminal, China's First Smart Terminal

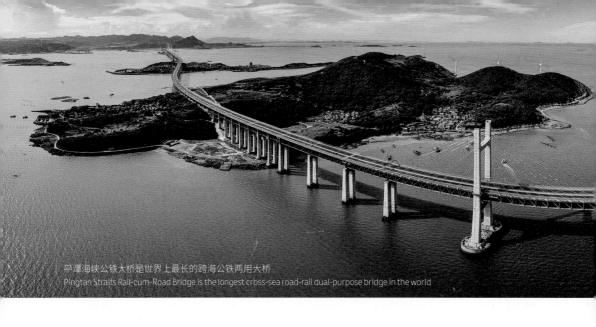

平潭海峡公铁大桥是世界上最长的跨海公铁两用大桥
Pingtan Straits Rail-cum-Road Bridge is the longest cross-sea road-rail dual-purpose bridge in the world

福州渔（溪）平（潭）互通交通枢纽
Fuzhou Yuxi Pingtan Interchange Transportation Hub
(photographed by Nian Wangshu)

泉州湾跨海大桥
Quanzhou Bay Cross Sea Bridge

福高铁动车
efu High Speed Rail High Speed Train

福州长乐国际机场
Fuzhou Changle International Airport

福州长乐国际机场
Fuzhou Changle International Airport

闽台融合
INTEGRATION OF FUJIAN AND TAIWAN

福建与台湾渊源深厚，往来密切，两岸开放交流 36 年来，福建发挥先行先试的作用，不断深化闽台合作交流，增进两岸同胞亲情和福祉，在对台交流合作中取得显著成果，已成为台商投资大陆的重要聚集地、重要的对台贸易口岸、台胞出入大陆的重要通道和两岸交流交往的重要基地，为推动两岸关系和平发展作出了重要的贡献。

今天，福建正发挥独特优势，先行先试，努力探索两岸融合发展新路，突出以通促融、以惠促融、以情促融，加快建设台胞台企登陆的"第一家园"，打造两岸融合发展示范区。

2022 年 7 月 12 日，第二十届海峡青年论坛在厦门召开
The 20th Straits Youth Forum adopts the theme of "Together for a Shared Future, Joint Efforts for Rejuvenation"

| 2018 年 8 月 5 日，金门各界人士代表共启通水阀门，福建向金门正式供水
On August 5, 2018, representatives from all walks of life in Kinmen opened the water valve, and Fujian officially supplied water to Kinmen

Fujian and Taiwan have strong ties and close interactions. In the 36 years since the opening of cross-Strait exchanges, Fujian has played a pioneering role in deepening cooperation and exchanges between Fujian and Taiwan, enhancing the affection and well-being of compatriots on both sides of the Taiwan Strait, and achieving remarkable results in exchanges and cooperation with Taiwan. It has become an important hub for Taiwan investors in mainland China, an important trade port with Taiwan, an important channel for Taiwanese to enter and exit mainland China, and an important base for cross-Strait exchanges. It has made great contributions to the peaceful development of the

闽台对渡泼水节，邯江与鹿港乡亲竞舟泼水，祈求海上安宁

At the Cross-Strait Water- Sprinkling Festival, folks from Hanjiang Quanzhou and Lukang Taiwan sprinkled water at each other to pray for peace on the sea.

福建文化宝岛行

Fujian Cultural Tour in Taiwan

relations between the two sides of the Taiwan Strait.

Today, Fujian is making full use of its unique advantages, conducting pilot projects to explore new paths for cross-Strait integration and development, focusing on promoting integration through direct links, real benefits, and emotions, accelerating the construction of the "first home" for Taiwanese and Taiwanese enterprises, and creating a demonstration zone for cross-Strait integration and development.

港澳合作
COOPERATION WITH HONG KONG AND MACAO

福建与港澳历史渊源深厚，地缘相近、人缘相亲。在香港居民中，闽籍乡亲达 120 万人，占香港总人口六分之一；澳门则有五分之一的人口是闽籍乡亲。乡情纽带让福建与港澳之间的经贸往来密切，香港是福建第一大外资来源地，港澳是福建主要出口市场和企业"走出去"的重要平台。福建与港澳之间已建立起经常性沟通交流机制和平台，推动经贸文化合作不断提质升级，走深走实、结出累累硕果。

Fujian, Hong Kong, and Macao have strong historical ties, close geographical proximity, and close friendship. 1.2 million of Hong Kong residents have Fujian ancestry, accounting for one sixth of Hong Kong's total population; whereas one-fifth of Macao's population has Fujian ancestry. This bond strengthens economic and trade exchanges between Fujian, Hong Kong and Macao.Hong Kong is the largest source of foreign investment in Fujian, and Hong Kong and Macao are important and main export markets and platforms for Fujian enterprises to "go global". Mechanisms and platforms for regular communication and exchanges have also been established between Fujian, Hong Kong, and Macao to enhance and deepen their economic, trade, and cultural cooperation, and yielded fruitful results.

以侨为桥 II

USING OVERSEAS CHINESE AS A BRIDGE

福建是海外侨胞的主要祖籍地之一，侨海资源优势明显，现有闽籍华侨华人 1580 多万人，居住在世界 188 个国家和地区。广大闽籍华侨华人爱拼会赢、恋祖爱乡、热心公益、造福桑梓，为福建和当地社会经济发展作出了重大贡献。据不完全统计，改革开放以来，全省引进侨资项目企业 36000 多家，实际利用侨资超过 1000 亿美元。侨捐累计达 300 多亿人民币。

福建坚持以侨为"桥"、为侨搭"桥"，团结凝聚海内外侨界力量，促进更多侨资、侨智、侨力汇聚福建，助力福建高质量发展。福建成功举办世界闽商大会、首届中国侨商投资大会、RCEP 青年侨商创新创业峰会等，广大侨胞在畅通国内国际双循环中发挥了重要作用。

| 2022 年 6 月，第七届世界闽商大会在福州举行
The 7th World Fujian-origin Entrepreneurs Conference was held in Fuzhou in June 2022.

| 2021 年 9 月，首届"中国侨商投资（福建）大会"在福州举行
The first "Overseas Chinese Entrepreneurs Investment (Fujian) Conference" was held in Fuzhou in September 2021

| 海外华侨陈嘉庚先后在厦门创办了集美学村、厦门大学
Tan Kah Kee,an Overseas Chinese, successively founded Jimei School Village and Xiamen University in Xiamen.

As one of the main ancestral places for overseas Chinese, Fujian possesses obvious advantages in terms of overseas Chinese resources. At present, there are more than 15.8 million overseas Chinese with Fujian ancestry living abroad in 188 countries and regions. The vast number of overseas Chinese with Fujian ancestry who worked hard, love their hometown, and are keen on public welfare have made significant contributions to the social and economic development of Fujian and the surrounding area. Available data show that, since the reform and opening up, Fujian has introduced more than 36,000 enterprises with overseas Chinese investment projects, utilizing more than USD 100 billion in overseas Chinese investment. Besides, donations from overseas Chinese have reached more than RMB 30 billion.

Fujian has insisted on leveraging overseas Chinese as bridges and constructing "bridges" for overseas Chinese. In other words, Fujian brings together the overseas Chinese community at home and abroad, and gathers more capital, wisdom, and talents from overseas Chinese to contribute to Fujian's high-quality development. The province has successfully hosted conferences such as the World Fujian-origin Entrepreneurs International Conference, the First China Overseas Chinese Entrepreneurs Investment Conference, and the RCEP Youth Overseas Chinese Business Innovation and Entrepreneurship Summit.

融侨集团参与投资建设江阴港
Rongqiao Group participated in the investment and construction of Jiangyin Port.

福建是最早实行对外开放政策的省份之一，近年来深度融入和服务"一带一路"，积极打造对外开放新高地。"海丝"核心区建设走深走实。全省累计设立外商投资企业 6 万多家，吸引外资 1400 多亿美元。2022 年福建省货物贸易进出口 1.98 万亿元人民币，与"一带一路"沿线国家和地区贸易额同比增长 13.8%。自贸试验区累计推出 563 项创新举措，其中全国首创 249 项，进一步完善具有福建特色的制度创新体系。海丝中央法务区加快建设，国际商事争端预防与解决组织全球首个代表处正式运营，知识产权 CBD 正式揭牌。中 - 印尼、中 - 菲经贸创新发展示范园区获国家批复建设。深化金砖国家新工业革命伙伴关系，进一步强化金砖国家紧密合作。21 世纪海上丝绸之路博览会、中国国际投资贸易洽谈会、跨境电商交易会等一批经贸活动影响力持续提升。

集装箱货轮从嵩屿码头驶离厦门港

Container ship departs from Xiamen Port from Songyu Port

21 世纪海上丝绸之路博览会暨第二十
届海峡两岸经贸交流会
21st Century Maritime Silk Road Expo &
20th Cross-Strait Economic and Trade Fair

As one of the first provinces to implement the policy of opening up to the outside world, in recent years, Fujian has deeply integrated and supported the Belt and Road Initiative, actively constructed new pacesetters of opening up, and expanded the construction of the Maritime Silk Road core area. Fujian has established over 60,000 foreign-invested enterprises and attracted more than USD 140 billion of foreign investment. In 2022, Fujian's imports and exports of goods reached RMB 1.98 trillion, and its trade volume with countries and regions along the Belt and Road increased by 13.8% year-on-year. Besides, a total of 563 innovative measures were introduced in the pilot free trade zone, including 249 pioneering measures in the country, and the institutional innovation system with Fujian characteristics was enhanced. Construction of the Maritime Silk Road Central Legal District was accelerated, the International Commercial Dispute Prevention and Settlement Organization established its first representative office worldwide, and the CBD for intellectual property rights was inaugurated. The state has also approved the construction of China-Indonesia and China-Philippines Demonstration Parks for Innovative Economic and Trade Development. The BRICS Partnership on New Industrial Revolution was expanded, and the cooperation among BRICS countries was further strengthened. The influence of economic and trade events such as the 21st Century Maritime Silk Road International Expo, the China International Fair for Investment & Trade, and the Cross-Border E-Commerce Trade Fair continued to grow.

| （上）福建自贸试验厦门片区喜迎五洲宾客
(Upper) Xiamen Area of China (Fujian) Pilot Free Trade Zone welcomes guests from all over the world (photo by Ke Xihui)

| （左下）中国国际投资贸易洽谈会，"丝路海运"展台
(Lower left) "Silk Road Maritime" Booth at the China International Fair for Investment & Trade

| （右下）东盟水产交易中心
(Lower right) ASEAN Fishery Exchange Center

新丝路跨境交易中心
New Silk Road Cross-Border Trading Center

国际交流

INTERNATIONAL EXCHANGES

福建与外国往来频繁，经贸联系密切、文教交流活跃，对外交往遍及五大洲。自 1980 年 10 月福州市与日本长崎市缔结首对国际友好城市以来，截至 2022 年，福建已与 46 个国家的省、市建立了 121 对国际友城关系，为双方民间交流交往搭建起重要平台。

福建积极举办海上丝绸之路国际艺术节、旅游节、电影节、中国福建周等国际交流活动，建设福建文化海外驿站、福建旅游海外推广中心，同海外友好国家和地区开展多领域的交流与合作。加大菌草、旱稻等援外工作，将菌草技术推广至 106 个国家。加强国际抗疫合作，组建医疗专家跨出国门协助抗疫。

（上）2017 年 6 月，金砖国家政党、智库和民间社会组织论坛在福州举行
(Upper) The BRICS Political Parties, Think Tanks and Civil Society Organizations Forum was held in Fuzhou on June 2017

（左下）2018 年 5 月，21 世纪海上合作委员会召开第一次全体会员大会
(Lower left) The First General Assembly of the 21st-Century Maritime Cooperation Committee was held in May 2018

（右下）第五届"海上丝绸之路"（福州）国际旅游节
(Lower right) The 5th Maritime Silk Road International Tourism Festival

Fujian has strong economic and trade ties, as well as active cultural and educational exchanges with foreign countries. In October 1980, Fuzhou established sister city relationship with Nagasaki, Japan.By 2022, Fujian had established 121 pairs of international sister city relationships with provinces and cities from 46 countries, providing a significant platform for intercultural exchanges.

Fujian has actively hosted international exchange activities, such as the Maritime Silk Road International Arts Festival, Tourism Festival, Film Festival, and Fujian (China) Week, established the Fujian Cultural Overseas Station and Fujian Tourism Overseas Promotion Center, and carried out exchanges and cooperation with friendly countries and regions in multiple fields. Besides, Fujian has increased its efforts in foreign aid in areas such as the breeding of fungi with herbaceous plants (Juncao technology) and that of upland rice, promoted the Juncao technology to 106 countries, strengthened international cooperation in the fight against pandemic.

2015 年 2 月舞剧《丝海梦寻》在美国联合国总部演出，反响热烈
In February 2015,dance drama "Pursuit of Dreams on the Maritime Silk Road"performed at the United Nations Headquarters in the United States received heated responses.

抗疫医疗专家组与意大利佛罗伦萨 Santa Maria Nuova 医院同行交流抗"疫"经验
The group experts exchanged experience in combating the epidemic with colleagues from Santa Maria Nuova Hospital in Florence, Italy

2022 年 11 月，28 国媒体记者访问福建，在筼筜湖畔合影留念
In November 2022, journalists from 28 countries visited Fujian Province and took a group photo by the Yundang Lake

CITY
LANDMARKS

城市地标

福州
FUZHOU

福州，简称"榕"，是福建省省会，先后获得国家园林城市、全国文明城市、国家生态市、国家森林城市等称号，获评中国十大"大美之城"。

福州是国家历史文化名城，素有"半部中国近代史"之称的三坊七巷，走出了林则徐、严复等一大批近代著名人物；被誉为"中国近代海军摇篮"的福建船政，在福州马尾诞生。

福州有山有水有温泉，山在城中、城在山中，山在水中、水在城中，是一座泡在温泉里的城市，城区 139 条内河星罗棋布、碧波荡漾，曾被马可•波罗称作"东方威尼斯"。福州自古就是海上丝绸之路的重要门户，是改革开放后中国首批 14 个沿海开放港口城市之一，造就了"海纳百川、有容乃大"的城市精神。

福州 GDP 已突破 1.2 万亿元，经济总量位居全省第一，形成了纺织化纤、轻工食品、机械制造、冶金建材、电子信息等五大千亿产业集群，海上福州、数字福州、新型材料、海港空港、闽都文化等五大品牌正在加快打响。

福州市标——三山一水，市树——榕树，市花——茉莉花，市果——福橘。

Fuzhou, or Rong for short, is the provincial capital of Fujian. It has been awarded as National Garden City, National Civilized City, National Ecological City, and National Forest City, and as well as one of China's top ten "cities of great beauty".

Fuzhou is a national historical and cultural city, known as the "half of modern Chinese history" with Three Lanes and Seven Alleys. It is famous for its significance in the modern Chinese history, and was home to a number of notable modern figures, including Lin Zexu and Yan Fu. Fujian Shipbuilding Administration, known as the "cradle of modern Chinese navy", was born in Mawei, Fuzhou.

There are mountains, rivers, and hot springs in Fuzhou. The mountains and rivers are harmoniously incorporated into the city, and hot springs are widely available in the city. Due to its 139 inland rivers with rippling waves, Fuzhou was once called "Venice of the East" by Marco Polo. Since ancient times, Fuzhou has been an important gateway to the Maritime Silk Road. With an inclusive urban spirit, it is one of the first 14 coastal open port cities in China following the reform and opening up.

Fuzhou's GDP has exceeded RMB 1.2 trillion, ranking it first in the province in terms of total economic output. It has also formed five industrial clusters with each valuing RMB 100 billion, including textile and chemical fiber, light industry and food, machinery manufacturing, metallurgy and construction materials, and electronic information. Currently, it is accelerating the development of five major brands, that is, Maritime Fuzhou, Digital Fuzhou, New Materials, Port and Airport, and Mindu Culture.

Fuzhou is symbolized by the three mountains and one river. Fuzhou's City Tree - Banyan Tree; City Flower - Jasmine; City Fruit - Fujian Tangerine.

福州"闽江之心"全景
A Panoramic View of the "Heart of Minjiang River" in Fuzhou

厦门
XIAMEN

厦门，又称"鹭岛"，是中国东南沿海著名的国际性港口风景旅游城市，城在海上、海在城中，素有"海上花园"美誉。国家主席习近平赞誉厦门是一座"高素质的创新创业之城""高颜值的生态花园之城"和"现代化国际化城市"。

厦门作为海上合作战略支点城市，是中国最早实行对外开放政策的四个经济特区之一、金砖国家新工业革命伙伴关系创新基地、中国（福建）自由贸易试验区三片区之一、国家自主创新示范区、两岸交流合作综合配套改革试验区、国家海洋经济发展示范区、东南国际航运中心、两岸区域性金融服务中心等。

厦门拥有联合国人居奖、国际花园城市、国家生态园林城市、中国优秀旅游城市、全国十佳人居城市、全国文明城市等殊荣。

厦门市树——凤凰木，市花——三角梅，市鸟——白鹭。

Xiamen, also known as the Egret Island, is a well-known international port and scenic tourist city along China's southeastern coast. The city seems to be built on the sea, so it is also referred to as the Garden on the Sea. Chinese President Xi Jinping has lauded Xiamen as a quality city of innovation and entrepreneurship, a beautiful city of ecological gardens, and a modern international city.

厦门白鹭洲风光
Scenes of Bailuzhou, Xiamen

As a strategic fulcrum of marine cooperation, Xiamen is one of the four special economic zones that first adopted the policy of opening up in China, one of the three areas of China (Fujian) Pilot Free Trade Zone, the National Independent Innovation Demonstration Zone, the Integrated Pilot Reform Zone for Cross-Strait Exchanges and Cooperation, the National Marine Economic Development Demonstration Zone, the Southeast International Shipping Center, and the Cross-Strait Regional Financial Services Center.

Xiamen has received numerous honors, including the UN-Habitat Scroll of Honor Award, the International Garden City, the National Ecological Garden City, the Outstanding Tourism City of China, the National Top 10 Most Livable Cities, and the National Civilized City.

Xiamen City Tree - Phoenix Wood, City Flower - Triangle Plum, City Bird - Egret.

漳州
ZHANGZHOU

漳州地处福建最南端，是一座拥有1300多年历史的国家历史文化名城，是闽南文化生态保护区的核心区。荣获中国优秀旅游城市、国家森林城市、国家卫生城市、全国文明城市等称号。

漳州山水交融，通江达海，拥有福建省最大的平原——九龙江下游冲积平原，海域面积1.86万平方千米，海岸线长715千米，是著名的鱼米花果之乡。漳州是中国经济实力50强城市，正在大力实施"千百亿产业培育行动计划"。漳州是中国食品名城、中国钟表名城，是21世纪海上丝绸之路重要节点城市、中国12个构建开放型经济新体制综合试点试验城市之一和跨境电商综合试验区。漳州是台胞主要祖籍地和台商投资集中区。古雷开发区是全国唯一的台湾石化产业园。台商投资区是国内台资企业最密集的区域之一。全市实际利用台资位居全国设区市前列。

漳州历史文化遗存丰富，南靖、华安土楼群被列入世界文化遗产名录。漳州有"三宝"，分别是片仔癀、八宝印泥和水仙花。

漳州市花——水仙花，市树——香樟、相思树。

Zhangzhou, located in the southernmost part of Fujian, is a national historical and cultural city with over 1,300 years of history. It is the core of the cultural and ecological conservation area in southern Fujian, and has been awarded titles including Excellent Tourist City in China, National Forest City, National Health City, and

漳州博物馆、艺术馆、规划展示馆
Zhangzhou Museum, Art Gallery and Planning Exhibition Hall

National Civilized City.

Zhangzhou, surrounded by mountains and water and has easy access to the Jiulong River and the sea, has the alluvial plain of the lower reaches of the Jiulong River, the largest plain in Fujian Province. With a sea area of 18,600 square kilometers and a coastline of 715 kilometers, it is a land famous for marine products, rice, fruits, and flowers. As one of the top 50 cities in China in terms of economic strength, Zhangzhou is vigorously implementing the Action Plan for the Cultivation of Industry with a Value of RMB 100 Billion. It is also a city famous for its food and watches in China, an important node city on the 21st century Maritime Silk Road, one of China's 12 comprehensive pilot cities for building a new system of the open economy, and a comprehensive pilot zone for cross-border e-commerce.

Zhangzhou is the main ancestral home of Taiwanese people and a hub for Taiwanese investment. The Gulei Development Zone is the only Taiwanese petrochemical industrial park in China, while the Taiwanese Investment Zone is one of the regions in China with the highest concentration of Taiwanese-funded enterprises. The city's actual utilization of Taiwanese investment ranks first among China's districts.

Zhangzhou is rich in historical and cultural relics; its tulou clusters in Nanjing and Hua'an have been included in the World Cultural Heritage List. The city is also known for its Three Treasures: Pien Tze Huang, Babao seal paste, and narcissus.

Zhangzhou's City Flower - Narcissus; City Trees - Camphor Tree and Acacia Tree.

泉州
QUANZHOU

泉州，古称刺桐，是唐朝中国对外四大口岸之一，10 至 14 世纪宋元时期，被称为"东方第一大港"；是古代"海上丝绸之路"重要起点、首批国家历史文化名城、首届"东亚文化之都"，联合国教科文组织授予"世界多元文化展示中心"。2021 年，"泉州：宋元中国的世界海洋商贸中心"被列入《世界遗产名录》。拥有世界级"非遗"名录 6 个、国家级"非遗"名录 36 个、国家级重点文物保护单位 44 处，是全国唯一拥有联合国教科文组织全部三大类别非遗名录的城市。

泉州是"晋江经验"的发源地、实践地，民营经济发达，经济总量破万亿元，在国内排名第 19 位，形成纺织服装、鞋业、石油化工、机械装备、建材家居、食品饮料、工艺制品、纸业印刷、电子信息 9 个千亿产业集群，上市企业 113 家，中国驰名商标 159 件。荣膺国际花园城市、全国卫生城市、国家生态市，是一座充满活力、独具魅力、温馨和谐的宜居城市。

泉州市树——刺桐树，市花——刺桐花、含笑。

Quanzhou, historically known as Citong, was one of the four most important ports for foreign trade during the Tang Dynasty. During the Song and Yuan Dynasties from the 10th century to the 14th century, it was known as the largest port in the East. Now, it is known as the starting point of the ancient Maritime Silk Road, one of the first batch of national historical and cultural cities, and the first Culture City of East Asia, and has been awarded by UNESCO the title of World Multicultural Exhibition Center. In 2021, Quanzhou: Emporium of the World in Song-Yuan China was included in the *World Heritage List*. Quanzhou also has six world-class cultural heritage and 36 national cultural heritage included in the list of intangible cultural heritage, as well as 44 national cultural heritage safeguarding units. It is the only city in China that has heritage included in all three UNESCO's lists of intangible cultural heritage.

Quanzhou is the birthplace and center of the Jinjiang Experience. With an economic aggregate of over RMB one trillion, its private economy can be said to be developed, placing the city 19th in China. Quanzhou has formed nine industrial clusters with each valuing RMB 100 billion in industries such as textile and clothing, footwear, petrochemical engineering, machinery equipment, building materials, household supplies, food and beverage,

泉州东湖公园
Quanzhou East Lake Park

craft works, paper printing, and electronic information. There are a total of 113 listed enterprises and 159 well-known Chinese trademarks. Quanzhou has been awarded titles including International Garden City, National Health City, and National Ecological City. It is a charming, warm, and peaceful city that is lively and suitable for residence.

Quanzhou's City Tree - Coral Tree; City Flowers - Coral Flower and Banana Shrub.

三明
SANMING

福建的母亲河——闽江发源于三明，在三明万寿岩发现的古人类遗址，被称为"闽人之源"。三明还是全球客家人公认的客家祖地。

三明全域都是中央苏区，"风展红旗如画"是三明的厚重名片。三明是新中国建设的新兴工业城市，"工业基地·活力新城"是人们对三明最深刻的印记。"中国绿都·最氧三明"品牌闻名遐迩，被评为国家森林城市、全国生态保护与建设典型示范区，也是国务院批准建立的全国集体林区改革试验区，国家林业和草原局确定的全国集体林业综合改革试验区和全国唯一的海峡两岸现代林业合作实验区。三明是全国群众性精神文明创建的发源地，"满意在三明"活动成为城市文明品牌，医改、林改、"金改"等改革走在全国前列。

三明市树——黄花槐、红花紫荆，市花——三角梅、迎春花。

全国文明城市三明
Sanming, a National Civilized City

Sanming is where the Min River, the mother river of Fujian, begins. The ancient human site found at the Wanshouyan Site in Sanming is referred to as the origin of Fujian people, and Sanming is also known as the ancestral home of the Hakka people around the world.

The entirety of Sanming City is part of the Central Revolutionary Base, making its name with the red revolutionary and glorious history. Sanming is a newly constructed industrial city in new China, and can be best described as an industrial base and a dynamic new city. It is also known as the city with the highest concentration of oxygen in China. It has been awarded titles including National Forest City, and National Ecological Protection and Construction Demonstration Area. Besides, it is a national pilot zone for the collective forest area reform approved by the State Council, a national pilot zone for comprehensive reform of collective forestry determined by the National Forestry and Grassland Administration, and the only cross-Strait modern forestry cooperation experimental zone in China. Sanming is the birthplace of the public's cultural-ethical standards. Its "Satisfaction in Sanming" campaign has also become a trademark of its urban civilization, moving it to the forefront of reforms including medical reform, forestry reform, and financial reform.

Sanming's City Trees - Yellow Locust and Red Bauhinia; City Flowers - Triangle Plum and Winter Jasmine.

莆田
PUTIAN

莆田，又称"荔城"，史称"兴化"，是"海上和平女神"妈祖的故乡、妈祖文化的发祥地。

莆田有国家旅游度假区、国家5A级旅游景区湄洲岛，全国首批示范河湖、全国十大"最美家乡河"木兰溪，列入首批世界灌溉工程遗产名录的木兰陂，被明代大旅行家徐霞客称为"福建三绝"之一的九鲤湖，汉族地区佛教全国重点寺院莆田广化寺，中国武术南拳发源地之一南少林寺，"中国江南三大古建之花"之一的元妙观三清殿等著名景区，有被誉为"宋元南戏活化石"的莆仙戏，有"春节一年两度""元宵一月欢腾"等独特民俗。先后荣获全国文明城市、国家园林城市、全国绿化模范城市等称号。

莆田拥有湄洲湾、兴化湾、平海湾3大港湾，40万吨级罗屿码头等一批深水泊位相继建成，是具有经济活力与开发潜力的一片热土。莆田工艺美术历史悠久、技艺精湛，先后获得"中国木雕之城""中国古典工艺家具之都"等工艺美术"国字号"品牌。莆田是中国跨境电子商务综合试验区，电商从业人员已达20余万人。

莆田荔枝、龙眼、枇杷、文旦柚"四大名果"驰名中外。

莆田市树——荔枝树，市花——月季。

Putian, also known as Licheng, historically called Xinghua, is the birthplace of Mazu, the sea goddess of peace, and the origin of Mazu Culture .

Putian is home to a number of attractions, including Meizhou Island, the national tourist resort, national 5A scenic spot, and one of the first batch of demonstration rivers and lakes in China; Mulan River, one of China's 10 Most Beautiful Hometown Rivers; Mulanbei Irrigation System, included in the first batch of World Irrigation Engineering Heritage List; Jiuli Lake, one of the Three Wonders of Fujian dubbed by Xu Xiake, a traveler during the Ming Dynasty; Guanghua Temple, a national key Buddhist temple in regions of the Han ethnic group; South Shaolin Temple, one of the origins of the Chinese martial art Nanquan; Sanqing Hall at the Taoist Yuanmiao Temple, one of the three famous ancient buildings in the south of the Yangtze River. The city is also famous for its Puxian Opera, the living fossil of the Southern Opera from the Song and Yuan Dynasties, and unique folk customs such as the celebration of the Spring Festival twice a year and the Lantern Festival lasting a month. Putian has been awarded titles including National Civilized City, National Garden City, and National Green Model City.

There are three bays in Putian, that is, Meizhou Bay, Xinghua Bay, and Ping Bay. It also has a number of deep-water berths, including the Luoyu Wharf, with a volume of 400,000 tons. Putian is a land of great economic vitality and growth potential. With its time-honored arts and crafts and exquisite skills, Putian has successively won national awards of arts and crafts, such as the City of Wood Carving in China and the City of Classical Art Furniture in China. Putian is a comprehensive pilot zone for cross-border e-commerce in China, with more than 200,000 e-commerce practitioners.

Putian's four famous fruits, that is, lychee, longan, loquat, and Wendan pomelo, are well-known domestically and internationally.

Putian's City Tree - Lychee Tree; City Flower - Chinese Rose.

莆田木兰溪两岸
Both Sides of Mulan River, Putian

南平

NANPING

南平位于福建北部，与浙江、江西交界，俗称闽北，是福建地域面积最大的设区市，有 4000 多年的历史，是中国南方开发最早的地区之一。"福建"之名即为福州、建州（今建瓯市）各取首字而来。

南平文化积淀深厚，是闽越文化、朱子文化、武夷茶文化的发源地。南平资源丰富，素有"福建粮仓""南方林海""中国竹乡"之美誉，粮食产量居全省第一位。

南平市自然风光优美、名胜古迹甚多。武夷山为中国四个世界文化与自然双遗产地之一，是首批国家公园、万里茶道起点。南平获评全国生态文明建设示范区、全国首个自然资源领域生态产品价值实现机制试点市、全国海绵城市建设示范市、国家森林城市、水生态文明城市、农业可持续发展试验示范区、森林康养基地试点建设市。南平以其优越的生态条件，成为全省唯一的以设区市为单位的国家级生态示范区，被誉为地球同纬度生态环境最好的地区之一。

南平市树——闽楠、香樟，市花——百合、桂花。

Nanping, located in the northern part of Fujian Province, is bordered by Zhejiang and Jiangxi, commonly known as Minbei (northern Fujian). It is the largest district city in Fujian Province, with a history of more than 4,000 years. It is one of the first regions in southern China to be developed. The name "Fujian" derives from the first character of Fuzhou and Jianzhou (now Jian'ou City).

Nanping has a rich cultural history, and is the birthplace of the Minyue Culture, Zhuzi Culture and Wuyi Tea Culture. It is also rich in resources and known as the "Granary of Fujian", "Forest Sea in South China" and "Bamboo Town of China", with the highest grain production in the province.

Nanping has an abundance of beautiful natural scenery and many scenic spots and historical sites. The Wuyi Mountains are one of China's four world cultural and natural heritage sites. Nanping is one of the first group of national parks, and the starting point of the ten-thousand-li tea road. Nanping has been awarded as the National Demonstration Zone for Ecological Civilization Construction, the First National Pilot City of Ecological Product Value Realization Mechanism in the Field of Natural Resources, the National Demonstration City of Sponge City Construction, the National Forest City, the National Water Ecological Civilization City, the Pilot Demonstration Zone for Sustainable Agricultural Development, and the Pilot City of Forest Health Care Base. With its superior ecological conditions, Nanping has become the only state-level ecological demonstration zone in the province with districts as the unit, and is regarded as one of the regions with the best ecological environment at the same latitude on Earth.

Nanping's City Trees - Phoebe Bournei and Camphor Tree; City Flowers - Lily and Sweet Osmanthus.

南平崇阳溪沿岸
Banks of Chongyang Brook, Nanping

龙岩
LONGYAN

　　龙岩地处闽粤赣三省交界，通称闽西。是全国著名革命老区、原中央苏区核心区，是毛泽东思想重要发祥地、古田会议召开地、红军长征重要出发地，享有红军故乡、红色摇篮、红旗不倒"三红"的美誉。龙岩是享誉海内外的客家祖地和著名侨区，是客家民系形成的核心区，全市80%以上的人口是客家人，长汀被称为"客家首府"，汀江被誉为"客家母亲河"。

　　龙岩是福建重要的矿区，已发现的各类矿产64种，其中14种储量居福建省首位。龙岩是福建三大林区之一。龙岩永定客家土楼被誉为"世界建筑史上的奇葩"，被列入世界文化遗产名录。

　　龙岩市树——香樟，市花——山茶花。

龙岩城区全览
A full view of Longyan City

Longyan, generally known as Minxi (western Fujian), is situated on the border of Fujian, Guangdong, and Jianxi Provinces. It is a famous former revolutionary base, the core of the former Central Revolutionary Base, the birthplace of Mao Zedong Thought, where the Gutian Conference was held, and an important starting place of the Red Army's Long March. It enjoys the reputation of being the birthplace of the Red Army, the red cradle of Chinese revolution and the home of the ever-flying red flag. Longyan is also the ancestral home of Hakka people at home and abroad, and a well-known region for returned overseas Chinese. It is a core formed by the Hakka people, as over 80% of the city's population is Hakka. Changting is known as the capital of Hakka people, and the Ting River as the mother river of Hakka people. Besides, Longyan is an important mining area in Fujian Province. The 64 types of minerals discovered, with 14 types of reserves, enables it to rank first in Fujian Province. Longyan is also one of Fujian's three forest areas. The Hakka tulou in Yongding, known as a wonder in the history of world architecture, has been included in the World Cultural Heritage List.

Longyan's City Tree - Camphor Tree; City Flower - Camellia.

宁德

NINGDE

宁德俗称闽东，集山、海、川、岛、湖、林、洞于一体，"海上仙都"太姥山、"亲水天堂"白水洋、"全国独有"鸳鸯溪、"名山奇峡"白云山、"海上天湖"三都澳、"华东第一瀑"九龙漈、"中国最美滩涂"霞浦滩涂等令人神往。尤其是被誉为"世界不多、中国仅有"的天然良港三都澳，是布局临港装备制造业的理想选址。

宁德是全球最大的聚合物锂离子电池生产基地和全球最大的不锈钢生产基地，锂电新能源产业作为继不锈钢新材料产业之后的第二个千亿产业集群，2022年产值率先突破二千亿元，2025年可望形成五千亿元产值规模。随着青拓高性能不锈钢新材料、1780毫米热连扎等不锈钢产业重大项目相继投产以及上汽、中铜项目的不断扩产，将为宁德工业高质量发展提供强有力支撑，加速宁德迈入"万亿工业时代"。

宁德市树——香樟，市花——桂花。

宁德东侨经济技术开发区
Ningde Dongqiao Economic and Technological Development Zone

Ningde, commonly known as Mindong (eastern Fujian), has well-integrated mountains, oceans, rivers, islands, lakes, forests, and caves, and boasts beautiful views such as the Taimu Mountain, the Fairyland on the Sea; Baishuiyang, a paradise of water; Yuanyang Brook, a national unique; Baiyun Mountain, a "famous mountain and strange gorge" ; Sanduao; Jiulongji Waterfall, the top waterfall in eastern China; Xiapu mudflats, the most beautiful mudflat in China. In particular, Sanduao, the only natural port in China, is an ideal location for the development of port-based equipment manufacturing.

Ningde is the world's largest production base for the polymer lithium-ion battery and stainless steel. As the second industrial cluster with a value of RMB 100 billion after the stainless-steel new material industry, the output value of the lithium battery new energy industry first exceeded 200 billion yuan in 2022, and is expected to reach 500 billion yuan by 2025. With the successive production of major projects in the stainless steel industry such as Qingtuo High Performance Stainless Steel New Materials and 1780mm Hot Rolling, as well as the continuous expansion of SAIC and China Copper projects, it will provide strong support for the high-quality development of Ningde's industry, and accelerate Ningde's entry into the "trillion yuan industrial era".

Ningde's City Tree - Cinnamomum Camphora; City Flower - Sweet Osmanthus.

平潭综合实验区

PINGTAN COMPREHENSIVE EXPERIMENTAL ZONE

平潭历史上就是东南沿海对台贸易和海上通商的中转站，清代咸丰年间被辟为福建省五个对台贸易的港口之一。平潭岛是中国大陆距离台湾岛最近的地方，规划建设的京台高速公路大陆段终点站和台湾海峡海底隧道北线入口都选址在平潭。

平潭综合实验区于 2009 年 7 月正式建立，是"闽台合作的窗口，也是国家对外开放的窗口"。2014 年 12 月，国务院批准设立中国（福建）自由贸易试验区。作为福建自贸试验区三个片区之一的平潭片区，定位为重点建设两岸共同家园和国际旅游岛。2016 年 8 月，国务院批复《平潭国际旅游岛建设方案》。自此，平潭形成了全国独有的"综合实验区 + 自贸试验区 + 国际旅游岛"三区叠加优势。

平潭区树——木麻黄，区花——水仙花。

平潭坛南湾旅游度假区
Tannan Bay Tourist Resort, Pingtan

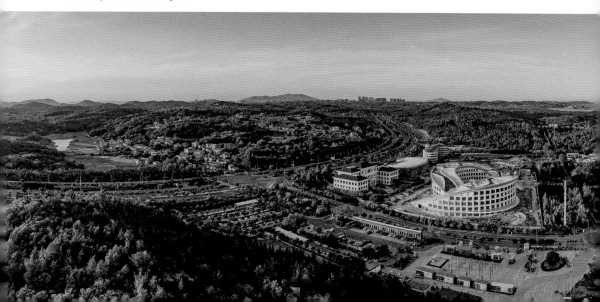

Historically, Pingtan served as a freight transfer station for marine trade between China's southeastern coast and Taiwan. During the reign of Emperor Xianfeng of the Qing Dynasty, it was opened as one of Fujian's five trading ports with Taiwan. Pingtan Island is the location closest to Taiwan Island from the Chinese Mainland. The planned terminal of the mainland section of Beijing-Taiwan Expressway and the northern entrance of the Taiwan Strait Undersea Tunnel are both located in Pingtan.

Pingtan Comprehensive Experimental Zone, officially established in July 2009, is the window of cooperation between Fujian and Taiwan, as well as the window of China's opening to the outside world. In December 2014, the State Council approved the establishment of the China (Fujian) Pilot Free Trade Zone. As one of the three areas of Fujian Pilot Free Trade Zone, Pingtan was positioned to focus on building a cross-strait common home and an international tourism island. In August 2016, the Construction Plan of Pingtan International Tourism Island was approved by the State Council. Since then, Pingtan has formed a unique combination of three zones, namely the "Comprehensive Experimental Zone, Free Trade Experimental Zone, and International Tourism Island".

Pingtan's City Tree - Casuarina Equisetifolia; City Flower -Narcissus.

清新福建

福来
福往

《福建概览》编委会

主　　任：张　彦
副 主 任：许守尧　陈添贵
主　　编：陈惠勤
副 主 编：陆传芝
委　　员：李静修　张思华　陈　澍

主编单位：福建省人民政府新闻办公室

策划编辑：赖小兵
责任编辑：辛丽霞　魏　芳
图片作者：吴　伟　阮任艺　陈映辉　张峥嵘　徐维耕　颜家蔚
　　　　　黄　海　吴国群　陈卫华　赵　勇　高忠锐　吴　军
　　　　　朱晨辉　王昌庶　张梓昌　夏日利　陈伟凯　卢鸣浪
　　　　　陈英杰　龚　健　赖小兵　吴寿华　严　硕　王沧海
　　　　　陈　奇　杨婀娜　陈长青　俞　松　吕　明　陆辅春
　　　　　念望舒　王勇华　王协云　游庆辉　庄灿枝　柯希慧
　　　　　黄立新　蔡　昊　陈秀容　林　璐　陈琦辉　刘利平
　　　　　林　书　陈卫华　王晓峰　张永艳　吴灵灵　施清凉
　　　　　（排名不分先后）

图片提供：大海峡图片库 福建省发展和改革委员会

版权与免责声明：本书部分图片来自大海峡图片库，作者署名及版权事宜未及落
　　　　　　　　实，请作者及时与我社大海峡图片库联系。
联系方式：0591-87538102
联 系 人：严　硕

Editorial Board

图书在版编目（CIP）数据

福建概览 / 福建省人民政府新闻办公室编 . -- 福州：
海峡书局 , 2023.4
  ISBN 978-7-5567-1105-5

  Ⅰ . ①福… Ⅱ . ①福… Ⅲ . ①福建－概况 Ⅳ .
① K925.7

  中国国家版本馆 CIP 数据核字 (2023) 第 067798 号

....

策划编辑： 赖小兵
责任编辑： 辛丽霞　魏 芳

....

《福建概览》

....

编　　者：福建省人民政府新闻办公室
出版发行：海峡书局
地　　址：福州市鼓楼区东水路 76 号 12 层
邮　　编：350004
设计印刷：雅昌文化（集团）有限公司
开　　本：787 毫米 ×1092 毫米　　1/24
印　　张：5
字　　数：96 千字
版　　次：2023 年 4 月第 1 版
印　　次：2023 年 4 月第 1 次印刷

ISBN 978-7-5567-1105-5

....

定　　价：88.00 元

Data of Cataloguing in Publication (CIP)

Overview of Fujian/ Compiled by The Information Office of Fujian Provincial People's Government —Fuzhou: The Straits Publishing House, 2023.4
ISBN 978-7-5567-1105-5
Ⅰ . ① Fu⋯ Ⅱ . ① Zhong⋯ Ⅲ . ① Fujian − Overview Ⅳ .
① K925. 7
China Version Library CIP Data Verification (2023) No. 067798

....

Planning: Lai Xiaobing
Executive Editors: Xin Lixia, Wei Fang

....

Overview of Fujian

....

Complier: The Information Office of Fujian Provincial People's Government
Publishing & Distribution: The Straits Publishing House
Address: 12 / F, No. 76, Dong Shui Road, Gulou District, Fuzhou
Postcode: 350004
Designed&Printed by: Artron Art Group Co., Ltd
Format: 170mm × 170mm
First edition: Printed in April 2023
ISBN 978-7-5567-1105-5

Price: RMB 88.00 yuan

....